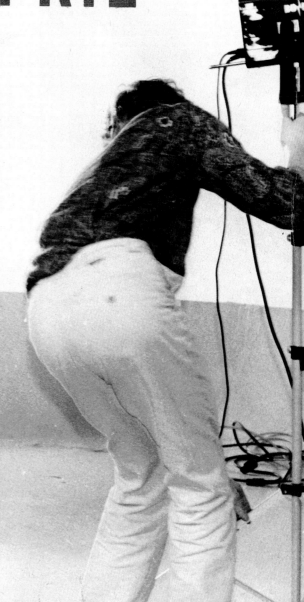

DOUBLE TAKES

For my father

DOUBLE TAKES

Anthony Grant

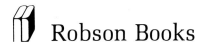 Robson Books

First published in Great Britain in 1987 by Robson Books Ltd,
Bolsover House, 5-6 Clipstone Street, London W1P 7EB.

British Library Cataloguing in Publication Data

Grant, Anthony
  Double takes
  1. Entertainers — Great Britain —
  Portraits
  I. Title
  790.2'092'2   PN2597

  ISBN 0-86051-455-2

Printed in Great Britain by
Butler & Tanner Ltd, Frome and London

CONTENTS

Acknowledgments

My grateful thanks to:
 Ilford for films and paper
 Paterson for chemicals and enlarger
 Wig Specialities for the hair
 Bermans and Nathans for the costumes
and *TeleTape Videos.*

Foreword by
H.R.H.
THE DUCHESS OF YORK

BUCKINGHAM PALACE

Over the last year, I have had perforce to undertake somewhat of a crash course in photography. I now understand a little bit more about its tricks and nuances; enough to realise that Anthony Grant has not only shown a high level of professional competence but has also discovered a most original approach to portrait photography. Whatever you think of his insight, its originality must be acknowledged.

I am delighted that proceeds from this book will go to help the Royal Marsden Hospital Cancer Fund; it is a generous gesture on the part of the author and will support one of the foremost British institutions engaged in the fight against cancer in every form. Anthony Grant's efforts in this direction must commend themselves to everyone into whose hands this book may fall.

Sarah.

July 1987

9

INTRODUCTION

At one point during the making of this book *The Sunday Times* asked me who *I* would have chosen to portray as an historical or legendary character. It was then that I realised I had set my sitters no easy task when I had asked them the same question. It was one of those cases when it is all very simple to come up with a plethora of ideas for everyone else until it arrives at *your* turn to choose. So I set to work and racked my brain, trying to present as honest an answer as I could.

Picasso? He had been the closest thing to an idol I had had for quite a time, with his seemingly limitless creative energy and his precocious ability to produce work that shocked by its genius and went on shocking (I had stood in awe before 'Les Demoiselles D'Avignon' in New York only weeks earlier). Then I read Francoise Gilot's book of her life with him, and the bubble burst.

John Lennon, perhaps, with his musical sensitivity sharpened at the edges with a wicked sense of humour? No. I read Cynthia Lennon's story and pretty soon that bubble burst too.

(I began to wonder if you have to be arrogant and self-centred to be a great artist.)

What about Beethoven? A giant among men. A genius whose soul mirrored life's darkest reflections with an awesome intensity.

No, I decided, I could not put up with that for too long.

Finally, I chose St Francis of Assisi. I pictured myself dressed in sackcloth, atop a mountain with only my dachshund, the birds, and myself for company, bathed in the radiance of the sunlight which warmed my face and soul, one small step from my maker (should I happen to slip!)

Of course being able to invent my own idea of St Francis was a great help – who can actually *prove* he didn't wear a sack and own a dachshund? The yawning gap of history, blurred with time, allowed me to think of him, not necessarily as he *was*, but as I *wanted* him to have been. And this is how the majority of people in this book approached the subject. I learned how little the average person (me, for instance) really knows about history and the true character of its most outstanding manipulators. I wonder if the great men and women of the past would even recognise the history books' portraits of them.

This restriction of our ability to know more than just a handful of sketchy points about those who came before us means that a book like this presents an enlightening glimpse of the sitters' own ideas (often distorted) of those people that they are representing. To watch ideas and inspirations forming in their minds before my eyes gave me hour upon hour of 'free performances' and, whenever the building up of a character, or more usually a caricature, occurred in front of my camera, I have included the whole sequence of pictures.

The inspiration for this book comes from one man and my memories of him.

In 1977, while I was still studying at art school, my father died from cancer. A month earlier he had walked across the South Downs, as outwardly healthy as you or I. He was 55 and I was 19.

Suddenly, after a space of a few weeks, he died. Many years earlier, near where he was walking that last month of his life, he had told me that once, when *he* was young and walking with *his* father, he had suddenly looked at him and realised that one day he would no longer be there, and been filled with a sense of dread and helplessness at this irreversible fact of life.

It had never crossed my mind that I would one day lose my father too. Fathers, I felt sure, go on and on, getting older and crustier, finally retiring (though with a great reluctance) to live on for ever more in their gardens and workshops.

No one I had ever known up until then had died and the idea of his not being there, anywhere, was something which I could not conceive. He was by profession a dentist and (together with my mother and sister) we lived in a house in South Kensington. He was always making things or watching others at their trade, asking questions and totally unsatisfied until he felt he could do the same job even better – which he always could, much to the chagrin of any calling electrician or plumber. I remember him making odd figures out of chicken wishbones and dental impression material. He would also let me run riot in the workshop with all the wax and plaster of Paris. I would build whole towns and villages in miniature on a table-top, and then blow them up with the gunpowder that I had pleaded with him to tell me how to make. He seemed to be able to build, draw, construct and mend anything at all – everything that had been put together was a source of fascination for him. All my interest in things of that nature comes from him.

The art school at which I was studying when he died was St Martin's in London's Charing Cross Road. I was part of the sculpture school. Some of the course consisted of photographing my work, so as to have a record of it, as it was usually then destroyed to make valuable floor space for the next 'creation'. I soon found that I had become more interested in taking pictures than in making sculptures and so parted company, one year early and degreeless, from this hallowed hall of learning.

Thinking that I knew all there was to know about photography (though in fact knowing next to nothing), I decided to pursue it as a career. I was blissfully unaware how many thousands of others have exactly the same idea, or I should have sold my camera and taken up pot-holing.

I sat waiting for my career to blossom – instead it shrivelled up and went away. I found myself with not enough pennies to buy a film.

So I took the nearest job to home, which was the post of X-ray porter at the Brompton Hospital, wheeling patients around in chairs. This, I thought, would give me money to obtain the equipment I badly needed. At that time I didn't have any cameras to speak of, save for an old Rolleiflex

12

twin lens reflex which my father had swapped his car for many years before. It needed a light meter, which I didn't own, and so could only be used with a lot of guesswork.

While working at the hospital, I started writing to a long list of people whom I wanted to meet and photograph with the idea of building up a portfolio and using my pictures of them to raise money in some way for the fight against cancer. To my amazement, within weeks I was confronted with a host of invitations to take photographs of people I had never really dreamed I would ever meet in the flesh.

My severe lack of photographic equipment did nothing to deter my enthusiasm at being offered such a chance. However, I was often met with looks ranging from concern to disbelief when I turned up to photograph such illustrious sitters as Henry Moore, Glenda Jackson or Lord Home with my hand-held old camera (O to own a tripod!) and burning-hot lamps atop a precarious home-made wooden stand (which actually housed woodworm). Once I had set up I tried not to move the arrangement of blazing lightbulbs again, as this invariably resulted in an explosion which did little to produce a relaxed expression on the sitter's face.

Once, on my way to photograph Harold Wilson, I was cycling in the Westminster area with my home-made light stand strapped to the front of the bicycle and all sorts of odd wires wrapped around me, when I was stopped by the police and questioned about my appearance. Being so used to travelling about like this I was at first baffled as to why I had been halted. I realised afterwards that I must have looked like some kamikaze human atom bomb heading straight for the House of Commons!

For those people who came to me to be photographed I obviously needed a studio, but I could not afford to rent one. Lying in bed one day I was suddenly hit by the idea that I would be just as happy lying on the floor and so I threw away my bed, along with everything else in my bedroom superfluous to my new career. I ended up with an empty room eight foot by eleven, which I painted white all over to give an impression of space. I planned to use this room until I could afford something bigger; however, most of the pictures in this book were still taken here. It has an

13

intimacy (so I'm told) that big studios have lost. There is nowhere for the sitter's attention to wander off to except into the camera.

Against the odds the results of my first pictures were not bad, and I was able to use them to entice more people to sit for me.

In 1983 I held a big fund-raising exhibition at the National Theatre in London. I had walked around several theatres trying, unsuccessfully, to find a venue for my work. Most were booked up for months, even years, ahead and were not all that interested in doing charity exhibitions. Finally, I strolled into the National and asked if I could show my pictures there, fully expecting them to say, 'No.' In fact, they did say, 'No.'

That evening, when I returned home, the telephone was ringing and I was told that the next planned exhibition there had fallen through and could I be at the theatre with fifty pictures, framed and mounted, in two days.

This is an offer you cannot refuse, thinks Anthony (hoping it is not also an offer he cannot manage). With money borrowed from everyone I knew I bought frames and printed night and day for the next two days.

The exhibition opened in the winter and stayed up over Christmas. My name appeared in lights ten feet high which danced their merry way across the front of the theatre for all the world, north of the Thames, to see.

At the same time I was doing a series of drawings with tenuous connections to various historical events and people that I thought would make good photographs. Expecting only some polite rejections, I sent the drawings to all and sundry and once again, to my continued amazement, the response was overwhelming. It turned out that many of those to whom I wrote had themselves, directly or indirectly, come into contact with cancer.

Through my previous work I had met a lot of actors and actresses, but I wanted my book to contain other people as well, from differing walks of life. I thought this would make it a stronger statement about everybody, no matter their varying backgrounds, being behind the fight against this merciless disease which now affects one in three

Galileo discovers the hottest part of the SUN

Galileo

Anthony Grant

people. I wanted to make it something above and beyond the usual book of celebrities smiling for some good cause, and I hope I've done it by choosing a list of people who perhaps you wouldn't find on the same bill for any other reason.

Of course everyone approached the project in their own way. Some took the whole thing in deadly earnest (though not many). Some, by the time I had arrived with my camera (and usually a wig or three), had forgotten what they were meant to be doing. Most just arrived and set about enthusiastically dusting off the memory of some deity here, or raising a long-dead tyrant from the dead there. All done, I must say, with a blissful lack of concern for accuracy or anachronism (rings, wristwatches and reading glasses abound).

I made all the sets (except Bob Champion's horse) and tried to create an atmosphere somewhere between gothic oppression and school-play optimism.

Recently I went to do a portrait picture of the wonderful A.J.P. Taylor. I showed him the pictures you see in this book and then, taking a deep breath, asked him if he would, as one of the world's great historians, like to take part.

'My dear boy,' he said, 'I am far too old for such games.'

I was of course disappointed until he looked up and said, 'But I do think they're rather good.'

Julie Walters as
JOAN OF ARC

'She was a total loony of course,' said Julie, as she struggled with the tangled braces on her chain mail trousers. 'Hearing voices and everything. She clearly was a schizophrenic, wasn't she?'

I cautiously raised my eyes heavenwards, expecting a thunderbolt to descend upon our wicked little scene at any moment. I toyed with the idea that either God was considering the validity of Julie's unorthodox theory or He felt the destruction of my bedroom to be just the sort of show of disdain He had given up since the Old Testament had ended.

'I think I look quite attractive, don't you? Rather glamorous, actually.' (A quick twirl in front of the mirror.) With a clanking of metal she picked up the breast-plate.

'What are these dangly bits? Are they to protect a girl's bottom?'

'They go at the front,' I said.

'Well, really!'

On with the helmet. A clang as it hits against the sword. 'I've discovered where the ringing in her ears came from! It's deafening in here. Actually, it's a fab cossie, darling. I feel hugely inspired, rather warlike. I look bloody terrifying! I think I'll wear this armour to go home in – God help the taxi driver who messes with me!'

'Right – lots of mad listening required now.' Adopting a truly heart-rending pose she knelt before me on the carpet, alert and inquisitive – lost in a private world where the unearthly voices of heaven descended upon her. She raised a hand to her ear...

'Come again... Do what?'

Slowly, with increasing force, the voices continued unrelentingly in her head. The angels came to her with such heavenly suggestions as 'Slay the English' and 'When did you last polish your helmet?'

The commands must have weighed heavily on her shoulders for, before my eyes, her head seemed to be descending inside her metal shell giving her the appearance of a galvanised turtle.

I feared for her sanity – had St Joan taken her over? She looked up at me from the carpet with glazed eyes and whispered, 'Isn't "Dynasty" on in a minute?'

Malcolm Muggeridge as
SOCRATES

Muggeridge lives with his wife Kitty in a long low farmhouse in the small town of Robertsbridge in Sussex. To drive a car there is to intrude upon the glorious silence that reigns in that area which, whenever I have visited it, seems for ever bathed in bright sunshine. Walking up to the front door I am very conscious of the violent sound of shoes upon gravel followed by the Muggeridges' terrible doorbell which grinds and screeches like a banshee.

'It has to be like that, my dear boy, otherwise I should have no hope at all of hearing my visitors.' I can see the idea mulling over in his head that perhaps this might not be such a bad thing.

He shows me how he can switch off his hearing aid should a conversation become too tedious. Then he needs only to nod and smile occasionally when it seems called for, serenely oblivious to his guest's stream of hot air.

But, I am assured, he likes me because I smile a lot and so he wouldn't dream of using such a ploy. Also the idea of playing Socrates is an unusual change from his daily routine. Kitty, who has made us some tea, finds the idea of Malcolm as Socrates quite hilarious.

'However,' she says in a serious tone, reinforced by a firm hand upon my arm, 'time merely repeats itself over and over again. I'm sure there was a Muggeridge in Socrates' time and you can bet there is a Socrates in Muggeridge's time. Would you like a biscuit?'

As we sat talking in his room, my eyes wandered about the place, over books piled layer upon layer from floor to ceiling, across his cluttered desk which strained under the weight of a dozen pieces of unfinished work, down to the old carpet (which complements his own marvellously wrinkled face and twinkling blue eyes) and out through the window to the garden now being tended in earnest by Kitty who seems to be in every room *and* the garden all at once, moving as silently and graciously as a butterfly.

But what of Socrates?

'Well,' said Malcolm, 'he was one of the big names wasn't he? A fairly bright chap.' Only Muggeridge could

24

sum up the father of philosophy in such a wonderfully ridiculous sentence.

'As for his similarity to me, that's not so easy.' (Malcolm, I'm sure, revels in pretending not to be a fairly bright chap himself.) 'He was willing to drink poison rather than compromise his beliefs – I hope I would do that.'

'I hope it never comes to that,' I said.

'At my age, dear boy, I don't think it would make much difference. You reach a time of life when you're like an old car that needs a new carburettor or new tyres every so often – things begin to wear out. You learn to relax, though, because you realise that you are not going to change the world any more and so you can just sit back and let it go on without you.'

He sat back and thought for a minute.

'Of course, like me, Socrates was terribly ugly, so I suppose I'm the right person to do him.' He laughed and twinkled his eyes.

Richard Briers as
CASSIUS

'I've chosen a tragic figure. Every comedy actor wants to do tragedy – it's in the blood.

'I played Hamlet in the early '50s and Richard III in the '70s – that's a gap of twenty years, which shows how good I must have been. Don't you think I've got the face for this?' said Richard, casting a sideways glance in the mirror. 'The long nose, the tortured lean and hungry look. Ah yes, this is the stuff.'

He raised his cupped hand to his mouth. 'Come in, Peter Hall.'

'Brutus is the famous one but you know it was Cassius who was the brains behind it. He was the plotter, and poor old Brutus was a bit of a reluctant old dear – roped in at the last minute. He'd much rather have stayed at home.

'We should have a picture of me taken from below, my raised sword about to descend on old Julius who has already been stabbed by all the others.'

I couldn't help thinking that if Cassius had looked like this, then Caesar would have had a job suppressing his laughter at the sight.

Richard obligingly climbed into a column I had made – I wanted to photograph him looking like one of the marble busts in the British Museum. We fell about laughing at the sight of him in his concrete mini-skirt, from which descended two very twentieth-century legs clad in shoes and socks.

'I look more like a corkscrew,' he said when I showed him the Polaroid.

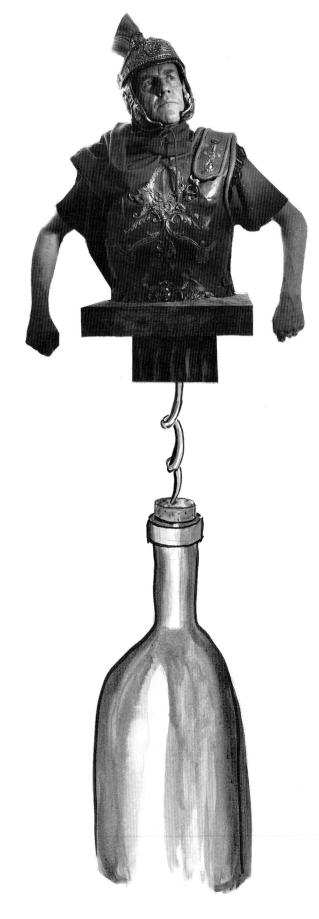

28

John Cleese as
LADY JANE GREY

'I suppose I am drawn to Lady Jane because she was such a complete prat.'

Succinct and certainly to the point, the concise Cleese potted history book, should it ever be written, may well be a little too direct for your average historian.

So here was I, on a hot July morning in a Bayswater Road office wondering how to transform this six-foot-three bearded Python into a petite adolescent about to undergo the painful separation of head from milky-white neck. The answer was simple – it's impossible!

'I don't have to take my trousers off, do I?' asked Cleese, struggling to ease the blood-red dress over his formidable frame. 'Only you see I've been swimming and I'm afraid I'm not wearing any underpants.' (Barely suppressed giggling from the direction of the two secretaries.)

'Right, I suppose I ought to look frightened or something,' he said, and proceeded to pull a series of terror-stricken expressions which would surely have torn at the heart-strings of even the most unfeeling executioner, resulting in an immediate pardon and a rewrite of history.

There is a large window at the front of John's ground-floor office. Every so often a passerby would glance in casually, and then do a double take at the man with full beard and off-the-shoulder Tudor dress kneeling on the carpet and pulling his face into a frantic series of tortured expressions. I was hidden from view behind a potted plant, giving the poor hapless observer a most unusual scene to ponder over as he went on his way down the road.

'And when is this calendar coming out?' asked Cleese, between grimaces.

'Calendar?' I said.

'Oh, of course – it's ten o'clock. You're the book. The

29

calendar is at eleven.'

And then it was done and the dress was on the floor and John was running off up the street to get something from his house. I packed up, said thank you to the secretaries, and left just as another man walked past me through the doorway.

'Ah, the calendar,' I thought to myself.

Jeremy Irons as
VINCENT VAN GOGH

Stratford-upon-Avon! Home of the Bard. Magnetic target to hordes of tartan-trousered Americans. It was, toward this cultural Mecca that my small car rattled one fresh spring day.

I was looking forward to this photograph. Somehow the surroundings of this Shakespeare-sodden town breathe life into any artistic venture and give one a sense of vision of truly Elizabethan dimensions.

I had toothache – but I didn't care!

On my arrival I was shown to Trevor Nunn's office which was to be my studio for the day. ('Mr Nunn is out.') I set to work transforming it for a Van Gogh self-portrait.

There I was, putting masking tape all over the walls in a frenzy of abandon, when a thin figure in dark glasses peered round the door. The man Irons!

He looked at some of the other pictures from the book and then set to work on the adjustments to his costume – the hat was too broad and a button on the jacket was wrong.

He studied the painting with a near-painful scrutiny and rolled a bandage around his head. He tore open some cigarettes and filled the pipe which I'd found the day before among a mountain of antique smoking material in the King's Road.

'I don't really have a valid connection with Vincent, you know,' said Jeremy with the tone of someone owning up to a crime.

'What made you choose him?' I asked.

'Well,' he stroked his beard and glanced skywards. 'Being a cold day and seeing as how photographers do tend to go on a bit, and knowing how a friendly smoke can get you through while they adjust their lenses and fiddle with their lights, I felt Mr Van Gogh would enable me to keep warm, relatively deaf and gently puffing while the operation took place.'

Van Gogh

 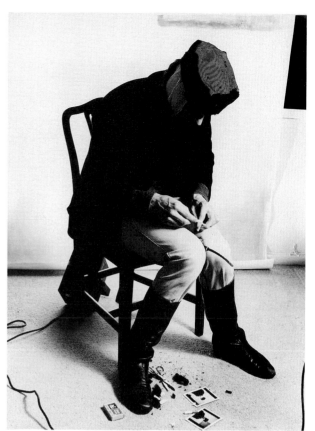

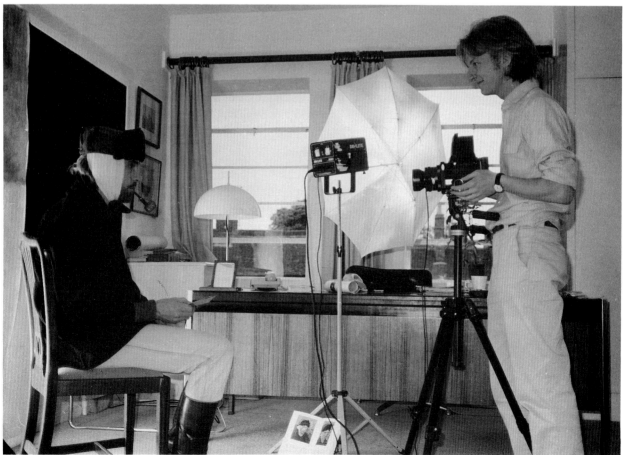

Mary Whitehouse as
BOADICEA

Along the A12 to Colchester. All the way to Mary's pink house in Ardleigh.

We'd met once before when I did a portrait for one of my exhibitions and had first mentioned the idea of my book. 'I'd have to portray a crusader of some sort,' thought Mary. 'It's difficult to think who, though – I wouldn't really want to have been anyone else, I'm quite happy being who I am. How about Boadicea?'

I decided to do the picture as a sort of Boadicea/ Whitehouse mixture which I thought would be more funny. It's quite a trial doing one of these pictures in someone else's house as it means moving all their furniture around and causing complete chaos, but Mary entered into the spirit of the adventure and the whole thing was lots of fun.

She laughed when I urged her to come up with a more substantial link between herself and the Queen of the Iceni.

'Well, she was more hefty than me in many respects.' (I'm still not quite sure what that meant.) 'But, like me, she took on a mighty adversary. She was under more pressure than me, of course.'

She thought.

'I hope the similarity ends there, though, because she drove the enemy out so far, but in the end she fell and was destroyed herself.'

Boadicea
7.12.83
Anthony Grant

Samantha Fox as
QUEEN VICTORIA

'There is no excellent beauty that hath not some strangeness in the proportion.' So said Francis Bacon, presumably eyeing one of Samantha's distant ancestors in some long-forgotten Elizabethan tabloid.

'We were not amused at the attention given to our chest and so have now branched out into the gainful world of pop singing and wine-bars,' said the Queen to me when we met in one's studio.

On that day little Miss Fox (for she is indeed a short one) was spread across the centre pages of the *Daily Something* in an interview which told of how she could earn a gaspable amount per hour by removing her top.

'This sounds easy,' I thought and stood in front of the mirror removing my shirt some half dozen times. But, alas, though I carried out this operation with some zeal the money continued not to pour in.

'How does it feel to own such valuable assets as part of your own body?' I wondered aloud out of genuine curiosity.

'Actually, most of the pictures you see are old ones. There's only one bloke who photographs me like that now – and that's not very often.'

The paper said she earned more than Mrs Thatcher. Is this true?

'I don't know – what does she earn?'

Money, money, money. Falling into her lap with such a ridiculous ease.

What will you do next?

'Retire at 21 and be a businesswoman – after I've hang-glided across the Grand Canyon.'

Oh yes – I nearly forgot. Why Queen Victoria?

'Well, she was small like me. We have the same tiny feet.'

(She wiggled her painted toes from under the crinoline structure in which she was enmeshed) 'and she was terribly romantic you know; I am as well. However, I don't think I fancy having nine children,' she giggled.

Later Samantha was whisked away in a mini-cab. The following week, the same driver, a small man of advancing years and retreating hair, brought me the great Max Wall.

'Tell me,' said the driver in an inquisitive whisper, 'that girl I collected last week, she's famous isn't she?'

Maureen Lipman as
DAME EDITH SITWELL

On the evening that I took these pictures, Maureen had been held up in traffic jams for longer than even the calmest being should have to endure and the end of her tether had been well reached.

We agreed that this was not the best of times to discuss the merits of Edith Sitwell.

So, a couple of weeks later, I sent her the prints and she wrote back.

'First of all, the picture is sensational . . . when you consider what little we had in make-up and costume.

'As far as why Edith Sitwell. Well. Why indeed? You threw the problem at me and my mind went blank as to who I should be. I feel so of this era, not at all an old soul. And so limited by my "Mittel European" heritage.

'Who? Rosa Luxemburg, Golda Meir, some Biblical creature like Lot's wife or Naomi among the fields of alien corn.

'Then the picture of Sitwell flashed through my mind. Not because I feel close to her or particularly admire her work. Just because she was an English eccentric. Point of contact!

'And because she made a feature of her features. Where perhaps I try and soften my angularity to conform to the accepted pattern of "beauty", she thumbed her nose (and the rest of her face) at current fashion. She became her own self-image, which is strange but admirable.

'When I suggested it to you I think you immediately felt the same excitement at the prospect of a "wild" picture.

'I arrived hot and bothered at your doorstep. I remember the house was a bit cold and I certainly wasn't in a photographic frame of mind. But because it was you I

co-operated and soon began to see it through your eyes and once again the fun of dressing up and becoming "possessed" took over.

'The result is superb. Mazeltov!'

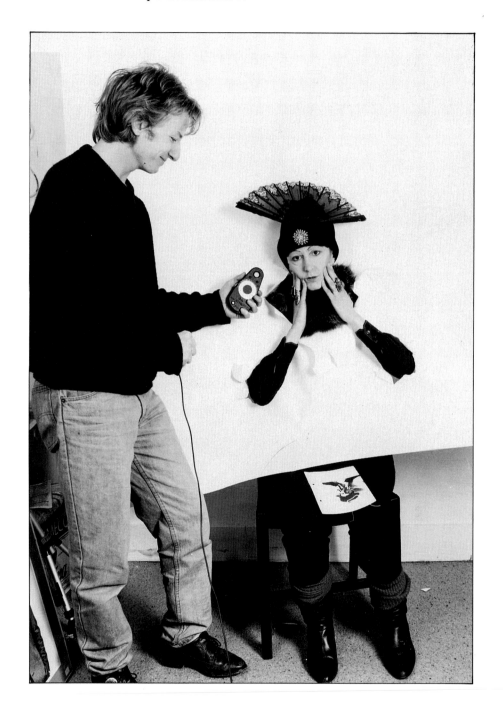

Max Wall as
KING CANUTE

'Difficult, difficult. Hmmm...'

The low voice on the end of the phone tapered away to nothing. I could sense him stroking his leathery chin.

'Historical character eh? Hmmm.'

(The last time I'd met Max he'd agreed to come over for an hour to do a picture portrait. We did the picture. More than two hundred pictures in fact. Five hours later, he still had my mother in hysterics as he sat telling her jokes and taking off her Scottish accent over tea.

Well, *she* drank tea. Max's tea consisted of Guinness and menthol cigarettes, each one lit from the one before. After that I drove him home and we went to the pub at the end of his road where he told me many funny stories in his often-imitated voice made of gravel.)

'I tell a funny joke about King Canute – take a picture of me as King Canute and print the joke next to it.'

A single spotlight picks out the solitary figure on the stage. He looks at the audience and starts to speak in his low voice...

'They told me when I was born I'd be rich and famous.

'Well – I'm rich aren't I?

'Well – I'm famous aren't I?

'Well – I was born anyway!

'Of course I'd never be famous like Henry VIII or King Canute – you remember him, don't you? Sat by the sea in an armchair.'

(He raises a hand and speaks in a quiet voice which gradually gets louder.)

'Back, waves. Back.

Recede, Ocean! Back, I say!! BACK!!!

'He was drowned, you know.'

Christopher Timothy as
ALAN LADD

'Do you mind an actor playing an actor? Because if I had to choose to be someone else it would be one of the great 1940s detective types. In moody black and white.

'Being a child of the Forties and an avid cinema-goer, my heroes were people like Alan Ladd, Robert Mitchum and Dick Barton.

'I grew up with those great images of cigarettes (no health warnings then), eye-shading hats, and the venetian blind that all the private eyes seemed to have in their offices; I'd have Lauren Bacall or Veronica Lake just outside the door, about to knock and beg me to find a lost husband, child, or dog!

'I think the picture should be me as a cross between Ladd and Dick Tracy. Very atmospheric. Great stuff!'

By strange coincidence Lauren Bacall was in London when I took the picture. I wondered if I should ask her to stand outside the studio door to add realism to the scene but, upon reflection, thought better of it.

Freddie Fox as
SIR FRANCIS DRAKE

'I feel a bit of a fraud,' said Freddie, hoisting up his drawers. 'I only chose Drake because my beard looks vaguely Elizabethan.'

But surely there really is a connection, I hinted. Loyal subject of the realm? Honest courtier to the good Queen Elizabeth?

'I suppose you may well be right,' he said, as though I were the first person to have pointed this out.

On the table next to him was an open newspaper with a picture from some horse race. Ascot, I think. There was a clutch of bonneted ladies watching the race and each other. Freddie's eyes lit up and he pointed to each hat in turn. 'That's mine, that's mine, that's mine. That's not mine.' He looked closer. 'Oh, yes, it is.'

In his costume he cut a dashing sight.

'I want to look as if I mean business – after all, he must have been quite a character to see off all those Spaniards.'

He glanced at the floor. 'Do you realize they've got this carpet at Balmoral?

'Yes, he must have been a lively man, perhaps even a little arrogant. How's this? I don't want to look too severe. Just a little frightening. Are my tights getting wrinkled?'

Jane Lapotaire as
CRUELLA DE VILLE

I remember first seeing Jane Lapotaire as Marie Curie on television when I was small, long before I had ever thought of being a photographer. I was struck by those wonderfully unusual features. They have been described by so many people so many times that I wouldn't even try. Jane has one of those faces at which I'd most like to sit and stare.

I first met her when she was starring in a musical called *Dear Anyone*, in which she played what I think is called an Agony Aunt. I took some portrait pictures which she used in *Spotlight*. She bought lunch for me in Sloane Square and said I could return the favour when I was earning £1000 a sitting. Needless to say, we still haven't had that second lunch.

Next time I took her photograph she was about to go onstage at the National in *Venice Preserv'd*, a rather heavy-going three-hour play in full Elizabethan voluminous costume.

'Not a lot of laughs,' she warned me.

So when I asked her whom she would like to portray, her answer was fairly instantaneous.

'Cruella De Ville!' she laughed down the telephone. 'That would make a change from playing St Joan. I'm always playing little grey mice or goody goody types.'

As I was taking the pictures, she explained her reasons in full.

'I've always wanted to wear long false fingernails and be draped in fur without feeling guilty. It's a new experience for me to feel good about feeling bad. And not to be corseted in the usual period costume. Do I look the Jungian archetype – or an advertisement for quick-dry nail varnish?'

What would Madame Curie have made of all this?
  'Ah, she'd have seen the vamp, the siren, the *witch* who
lurks inside all *good* women!'
  She held her arms aloft, claw-like nails ready for the kill.
  'I'll get you,' she screeched, 'and your little dog too!'

David Bellamy as
THE MISSING LINK

Isn't life wonderful? Just when you think that that skeleton you have in a box in the cellar is never going to be used for anything, along comes David Bellamy saying he'll be the missing link as long as he can smile in the picture and your brain starts flashing with ideas of the set you are going to build.

Your search for a room big enough to house the scene and end up commandeering your mother's bedroom and telling her you promise to leave it just as you find it and start building a hollow desk with a hole for the Bellamic Man's head, and repainting the walls and transforming it into a dark and dusty Victorian laboratory.

Meanwhile your long-suffering mother is reduced to sleeping on the floor and being confronted in her waking hour by a smiling skull which leers at her from its table top.

You build a glass case to house the famous naturalist's head but discover on his arrival that it won't fit around his neck and so you convince yourself that he looks better without it just as he gets cramp and your dog runs underneath the desk and starts barking at him.

'It's an astonishing set,' he says, straining to look about him.

'Yes,' you say, 'that was my sister's skeleton,' and he looks very surprised and not a little worried so you explain that you mean she is a physiotherapist and she *owns* it and when you say it was hers you don't mean it was *hers*.

Several films later, it's all over and you retire downstairs and drink tea together while your guest rubs the red weal that has formed around his neck and thanks you for taking his picture and wanders off in the direction of the Natural History Museum.

Isn't life wonderful?

Joanna Lumley as
HENRY VIII

Joanna is one of my favourite people to photograph – she is certainly one of the easiest to photograph and it is always a lot of fun. So when she suggested being Henry VIII I knew it was going to be an enjoyable afternoon.

I found a painting of Henry in the manner of Holbein and set to work painting a backdrop which had the same feel to it. I love the arrogant stance that he adopted in these pictures – defying anyone to stand up to him and try their worst. What a world it must have been.

I went to Bermans for the costume and luckily we found a strap-on fat belly which looked gloriously obese under the outfit.

On the day of the picture Joanna set to work transforming herself into the Tudor king. The beard went

on and the eyebrows 'came off'. But somehow her face just didn't look *square* enough. So in went some paper to the mouth. The spectacle was complete.

'I feel wonderfully *fat*,' said Joanna, head back in laughter, with hands on hips and stomach bulging through her costume. 'And fearfully arrogant.

'*Off with his head!*' she roared.

'Here we are all killing ourselves to go on special diets,' she said, peeling off her beard in the mirror after we'd finished, 'as if eating leaves makes you thin – hippos eat leaves, don't they? There is this thing about looking svelte and slim, whereas in those days' (she placed her hands on her stomach) '*wumph!*

'After all, variety is the spice of life. If you're fat, you're fat – actually I miss my cheeks already, although I'm quite pleased to have my eyebrows back and I won't be walking around with paper in my mouth! I think I looked rather cruel behind that beard and moustache – it actually made me feel quite different being fat – I enjoyed it! We wouldn't be talking about Henry VIII so much if he had been slim and attractive. A beach boy! On reflection, I think I rather like him as he was – after all, he did write "Greensleeves", didn't he?'

Dame Peggy Ashcroft as
LILIAN BAYLIS

I knocked on the dressing-room door at the Royal Opera House in Covent Garden.

A couple of days earlier I had had a telephone call from Peggy saying that she would be doing her 'Tribute to the Lady', the 'Lady' being Lilian Baylis, as part of a fund-raising venture to prevent the closure of the Sadlers Wells Theatre.

'I would like to portray Lilian in your book, so why don't you come to the theatre and do the picture there as I will be dressed in her original costume from the Victoria and Albert museum?'

When a small black-haired figure in gown and mortar-board opened the door, I though I had come to the wrong place.

'I'm sorry,' I said. 'I'm looking for Miss Ashcroft.'

'Oh yes, do come in,' said the smiling face. It took me a full twenty seconds to realise it was *her*.

She told me about Lilian Baylis, how she had founded the Old Vic and the many strange stories connected with her, including how she would openly insist to God that He supply her with enough money to keep the theatre going and how the money had miraculously appeared on her desk. How she would fry bacon and eggs in her private box during a performance and the smell would waft down across the audience seated below.

'Lilian's supreme gift,' said Peggy, 'was getting other people to do miracles for her. No one quite knew why they did things they would never do for anyone else.

'She would talk out of the side of her mouth, like this.

'Her famous quote was "I so believe the theatre is our greatest power for good or evil that I pray my earnestness may give me words in which to express this faith".'

I have been fortunate in my work to meet many people who are among the greatest exponents of their particular craft or profession. To meet Peggy Ashcroft, who is charming beyond description, was a great honour for me.

Ron Moody as
MOSES

'Nice material this man Moses wore,' said Ron, thumbing the robe I'd got for him to wear. I'd improved on the Bible, and produced a set of ten tablets – one for each commandment. God was economical, and used only two – He got all the commandments on by writing on both sides.

'I ought to look as if I'm struggling under the weight of all these stones. "Hey God, next time – do it *Yourself*".'

Down on his bended knee, with arms outstretched holding the tablets, Ron began to sing Al Jolson melodies.

'April showers...'

Before each photograph he would shout something out to help him make the right expression:

'But I didn't say that.'

'How many times do I have to tell you.'

'There was an eleventh commandment – but I can't remember what it was.'

'It wasn't easy.'

'Boy, did you get a wrong number!'

'Think anyone's going to listen?'

'Next time, I'll get it on two tablets.'

Moses

Bob Champion as
DICK TURPIN

Bob Champion is the man who fought cancer and won. His story is well known and I was particularly honoured when he said he would help me with my work. He has had celebrity rather thrust upon him and you get the feeling when you meet him that it's probably not something that he would have chosen himself. However, through his example, he has given hope to many others and has helped to further the cause of the fight against the disease.

'I suppose I ought to be someone who had a horse,' he said when he was thinking of a character.

I figured a horse might not fit that well inside my bedroom so, when he suggested being Dick Turpin, I travelled up to his stables in Suffolk.

Against the morning tide of commuters I left London at 7 a.m. and rattled along the A11 to Newmarket where I left the motorway and drove east to Timworth. It was a beautiful morning. Thermos, my dog, sunbathed on the passenger seat. I suggested he drove for a while and let me sunbathe. Being a dachshund, he pretended not to understand.

Bob had that week travelled the distance from London to

Aintree with the one time Grand National winner Aldaniti. Several well-known people, including the Duchess of York, had ridden the horse part of the way to raise money for the Royal Marsden.

When I arrived at the stables I was able to look around and see the horses at close range. They are wonderfully dignified with their majestic expressions and long powerful legs. By now it was a hot, clear morning, and standing in the wide open countryside I felt much further away than the hundred miles I was from London.

There was much hilarity among the jockeys and staff as Bob walked briskly from the house dressed as Turpin. In one move he was up on the horse and off trotting around the field. At first the horse was a little timid of the camera but between them both (and remember they are not actors!) I think the spirit of the Highwayman was re-kindled quite well.

Susan George as
GRETA GARBO

I first met Susan when I went to photograph her in her West-End dressing-room for one of my exhibitions. Simon MacCorkingdale was there, too, so I took photographs of both of them. They thought these were good and subsequently, when they got married, I was asked to do the photographs.

When I asked Susan to pick a character for my book she immediately chose Greta Garbo. I went to her house to do the picture and asked her about her choice:

'There was a tranquillity in her face no matter how she was being photographed or filmed, whatever mood she was in. She showed a great peacefulness and resolve, and she could also be very glamorous and exotic. There is a famous shot of her in a beret where she looks vulnerable and naive.

'I would like to have known her, and to know some of the stories that lay behind those dark eyes.

'To be a *star* in her era was really something special indeed. She let others deal with her "image" and, at times, I think this would be wonderful. But today the world is very different and you have to be able to stand up and talk for yourself, and be responsible for your actions. I'm far too out-spoken to be a silent type.

'Of course a lot of her legend was built up around the fact that she rarely spoke. In fact, her English was never very strong and she was no good at interviews. Hence the image was built of the obscure woman who had this vagueness with the world. But I do quite admire that obscurity.

'As for her face – well, it was a classic face. *My face?'* Susan thought for a second and laughed. 'It's too ill-proportioned, really, for Garbo. Hers was so well defined. I consider mine to be odd and quirky!'

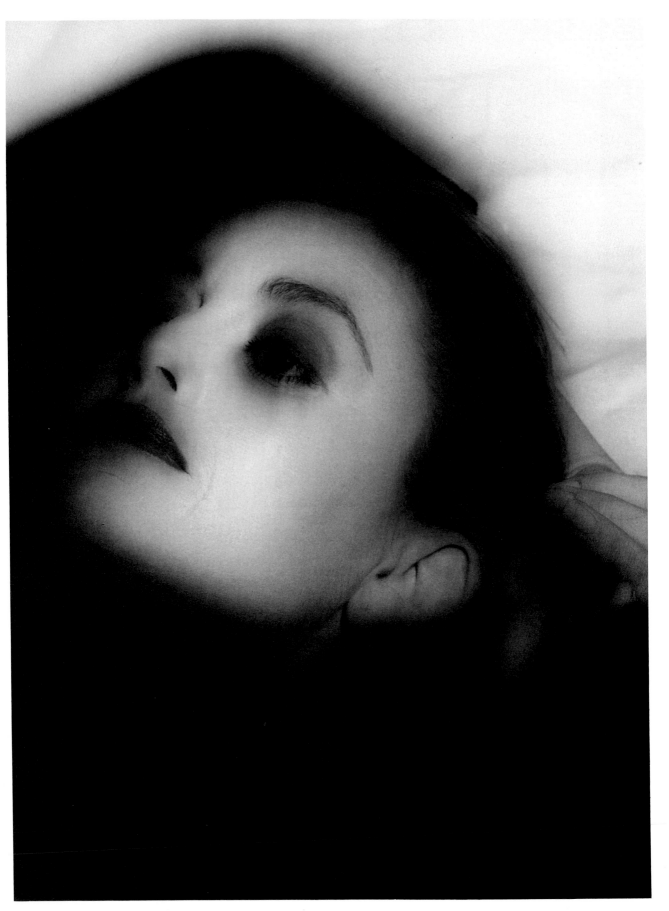

Sir Roy Strong
JUPITER

When I was younger we lived in a house opposite the Victoria and Albert Museum in South Kensington. Every Saturday morning I would go there and have a drawing lesson before the museum opened. There were about ten of us, maybe only eight years old, free to wander around the empty museum sketching the exhibits. So it was strange to go back, twenty years on, and hand in my letter to Roy Strong, the outgoing director.

He replied the next day saying that he would like to be Jupiter, and we arranged a date for the following week. He

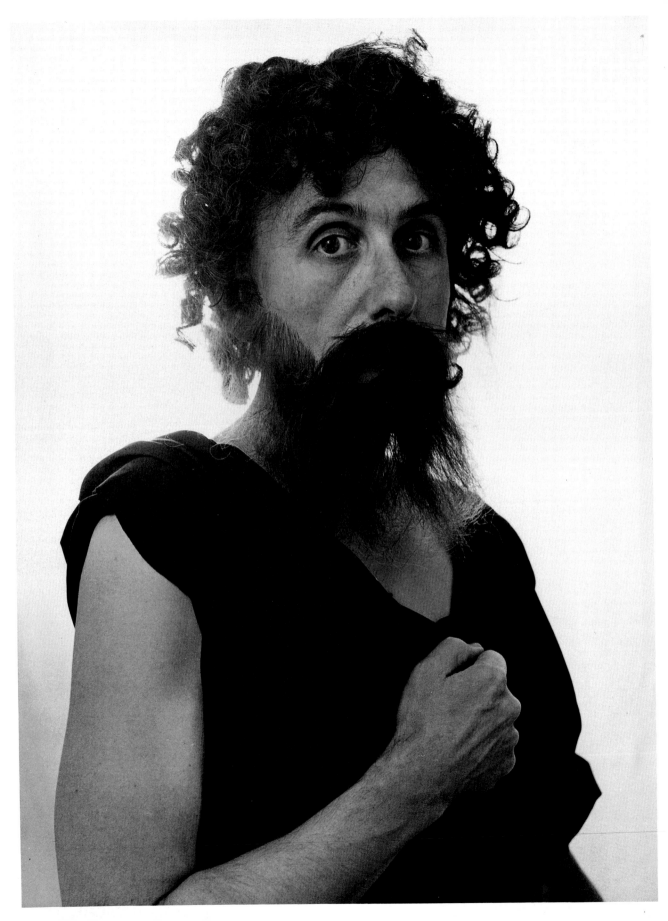

is a very precise man and I had plenty of warning from his office that I should make the photograph very authentic or he would be far from pleased.

So it was that we settled for a head and shoulders shot, concentrating on the face.

He looked at the Polaroid test shot.

'This has the makings of a good photograph,' he said, and I breathed a sigh of relief. (He had already told me that he was the most photographed director the V & A had ever had. Names like Beaton, Bailey, Snowdon and Brandt tripped off his tongue – 'I enjoy watching artists at work.')

'We need more of a plunging neckline – it ought to look like Julia Margaret Cameron's picture of Tennyson as Poet Laureate.'

I asked him why he had chosen Jupiter.

'Minerva,' he said. 'Minerva sprang from the head of Jupiter – the goddess of wisdom and learning. I'm a great believer in learning. I don't think I'd like to dwell on Jupiter's love life – I certainly didn't choose him for that reason. Jupiter was a chameleon – always changing and appearing somewhere else in a different disguise. I see myself in a multiple role, in the sense that everyone thinks they have pinned me down and I always turn up somewhere else doing something else.'

How would Jupiter have looked, I wondered.

'Commanding. Creative. Noble and majestic. Grand! But without any sense of humour, which is not really in character for me.'

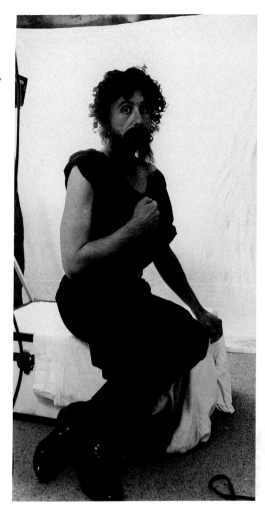

TEA-BREAK

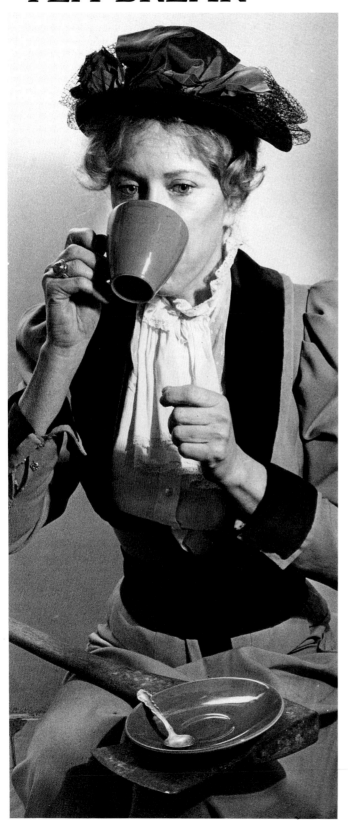

now read on...

Lindka Cierach as
EVE

Lindka is someone whom I first met at the time of the 1986 Royal Wedding, and she has since become a good friend.

Sitting in her house a week before the event, knowing that *that* dress was just up one small flight of stairs, did give me an odd feeling of being very close to something that was the centre of much attention – not to mention the feeling of pressure on its creator.

(Andy Warhol was the first 'famous' person I ever photographed and I often thought of his maxim about the fifteen minutes of fame – the strange time when it seems that the whole world has focused its eyes on you.)

Lindka's first reaction to my suggestion that she appear in the book was one of stunned incredulity that she should be considered famous enough.

A mere eight months later, there she was idly nibbling away at an apple as I changed films, proffering various theories on why she had chosen Eve.

'She was the first clothes designer of course – I like these dinky little fig leaves you've made, by the way.'

'It was nothing,' I said, thinking that in fact, now she was wearing them, that was practically what they looked like – nothing!

Loosening my collar I proceeded to click away – weren't those lights making it very hot in here?

'Also I would love to have long wild cascading hair like this – hair you can do *anything* with, that's a real dream of mine.

'And her power over men, that's a good reason to do her.' She threw her head back and laughed. 'She made him eat the apple didn't she? O, for a woman to have such power!'

I suggested that women do have that power and are poorly advised if they think otherwise.

Often the person I was photographing wanted to know about all the others I had done – what they had said and what had happened.

There was much falling about with laughter as I went through the list for Lindka. It was about midnight when we finished the session.

'Have you figured out what order they are going into the book?' she asked as we went to look for a taxi.

'No,' I said, 'but I think I may have decided upon the centrefold.'

Alan Coren as
HIAWATHA

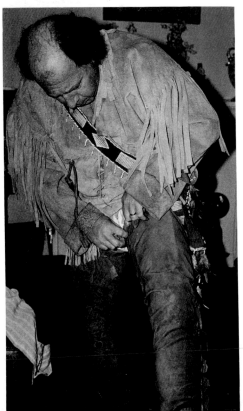

As he'd been editor of *Punch* for so long, I felt sure Alan would come up with a suitably ludicrous character.

He did.

'I've waited years for this opportunity,' he said as he struggled with his extremely unaccommodating costume. I was laughing at the sight of him lying down, wriggling back and forth with flaying legs as he fought a desperate battle with his suede leggings.

'Picture the scene,' he said. 'A six-year-old Coren on stage in his first minor role at the Osidge Primary School. The play was *Hiawatha*, but I didn't get the starring role because one of the other boys' mother knew someone with a farm so she was able to get real goose feathers for his costume. But me? No! I had to settle for a costume made of black-out curtains and a head-dress of putrefied chicken feathers held to my skull with Sellotape. The indignity of it!

'So this is my big break. The lead role at last. I feel I ought really to assume that pose you see in the pictures of all those Red Indians Custer captured who didn't know what a camera was (I'm not sure Custer did either). They would look puzzled and lost, yet still managed to retain their massive dignity and pride.'

'This is massive dignity and pride?' I wondered, as I peered through the viewfinder.

'Finally, they can stand no more. They retaliate! Die, white man! Bloody hell, I can't get my knife out of my trousers. No wonder they were wiped out!'

Brian Glover as
NIKITA KHRUSHCHEV

Brian's gigantic Yorkshire voice boomed around the studio.

'We need a connection!' he bellowed.

He thought for a moment.

'I was born in 1934...' (pause) '... my Mum went on a day trip to Vladivostok.' Laughter.

'She went with the Barnsley Conservative Women's Guild... I've always worried about this!' Guffaws.

'Was Khrushchev a Georgian? They're all Georgians, aren't they? Let's make it Tbilisi, it would be even better...

'I was born in 1934...

'... in August 1933 Tbilisi F.C. played Barnsley F.C. at home. And my Mum went!' Roars with laughter.

'She was chairwoman of the Barnsley Supporters Club.'

'And maybe Khrushchev was linesman,' I suggested.

'Ah, now. Let's bring in some Communism... I was born in 1934...

'... in 1933 a young Khrushchev visited Barnsley to meet Arthur Scargill's dad and my mother was very friendly with Arthur's elder sister...'

Dissolves in a hysterical roar.

99

Eamonn Andrews as
JOHN THE BAPTIST

'Could you fix it to put my head on a plate?' came the furtive reply to my letter. 'I'd like to do John the Baptist.'

I'd never suspected there could be such a gruesome side to the man with the sunny 'This is your Life' disposition.

Eamonn, as everybody nows, used to be a boxer and in his beard looked to me more like Long John Silver than the Baptist. However, the transformation was completed when he put on his wig, wild hair exploding in all directions. I often wonder what the people who live opposite me feel when they see perfectly normal people enter the house dressed in conventional clothes, only to appear minutes later at an upstairs window in chainmail or mediaeval robes or, that hideous twentieth-century invention, Y-fronts. On many an occasion someone in this book, while in a state of advanced undress, would cast a worried glance out of the window to check that the car hadn't been clamped, only to realise that half the windows opposite had faces looking out of them.

Eamonn duly took up his position with his head on the plate.

'Poor old John, it must have been rough.'

A truly British sentiment. Can you imagine it in the Bible:

'*Then at the celebration of Herod's birthday, the daughter of Herodias danced before them all, and Herod was so well pleased that he promised to grant whatever request she made.*

'*Give me, she said, the head of the Baptist, give it me here on a dish.*

'*Poor old John, it must have been rough.*'

'What were John the Baptist's famous quotes?' asked Eamonn's disembodied voice from his plate. 'That's the

trouble – we all remember the gory details but forget what the man said.'

'Wasn't it, "Ouch my head – no more cheese and Salome on an empty stomach"?' I hazarded.

'Something like that,' laughed the severed head.

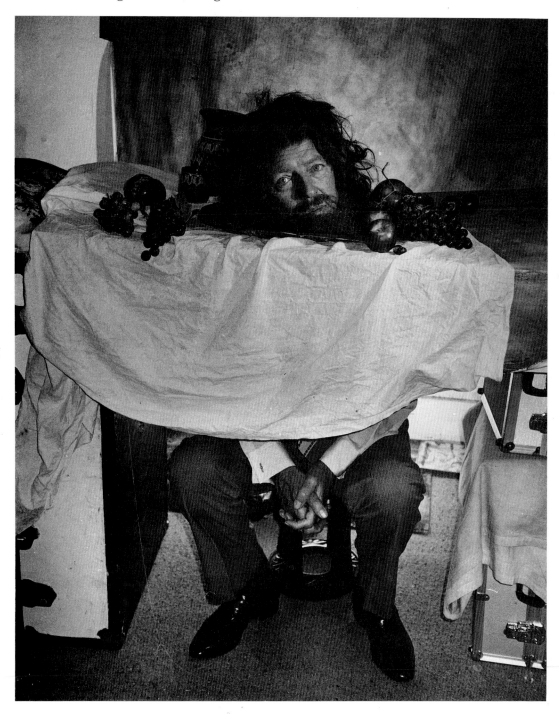

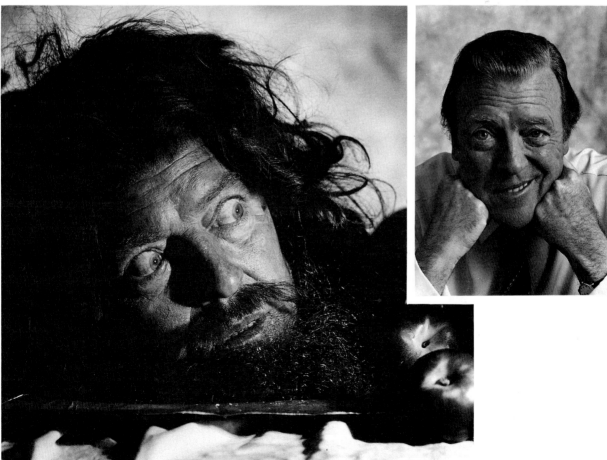

Susan Penhaligon as
THE FIRST WOMAN IN SPACE

'I've always wanted to know what it's like to sneeze inside a space helmet. I mean, where do you put your hanky?

'I could be chasing an unruly banana around the cabin – except they probably eat dehydrated banana tablets.

'This outfit is wonderful – can I have it? The silver boots, the light-reflecting trousers, a fashionable young woman's dream.

'Before astronauts take off they pose in front of a picture of the moon or the earth, don't they? Like this. Looking proud and adventurous. "I'll be up there soon," they say as they gaze up into the distant stratosphere.'

I met Susan two months later and showed her our combined efforts.

'I can't remember why I chose to be this character now,' she said with painful honesty. 'Was it something to do with recognising a woman's ability to do the same job as a man equally well? I think that was it – let the women have a go! And the pioneering spirit, of course. To be the first person to do something. There are few things left now to be the first person to do. Are these reasons interesting enough? They sound a bit boring to me. Let me think ... ah yes! ...'

She burst out into uncontrollable laughter and came up with a suggestion that I truly wish I dared to print.

Peter Egan as
HAMLET

'What can I say about Hamlet that hasn't been said? Hamlet is *the* part in Shakespeare. To tell the truth I don't think anyone's going to ask me to play it now – I'm too old! This could be my last chance to play that great hero. (You're not going to put that in your book are you? – It could be the end of my career.)' He laughed. 'Be kind!' he appealed.

'Seriously, though, there is a wonderful moment in the graveyard scene where he is whispering into the ear of the skull. It's such a famous scene – it's the one I'd like to do in the photograph. The magical moment when life looks at death and sees the separation between the two as being very tenuous indeed. How can this *thing* be all that is left of the man with whom he talked and laughed? It's a classic moment in theatre.'

And so it became a classic moment in my studio where life looked at death and death's spring snapped and its jaw fell off on to the carpet and the scene dissolved into very un-Hamlet-like laughter.

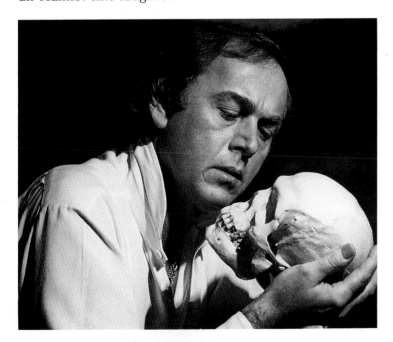

MIRROR, MIRROR...

Ten kisses ... er ... um ... er

How about "Ten kisses short as one,
one long as twenty —
leading him prisoner
in a red rose chain —
Love is a spirit
all compact of fire —
He sees her coming
and begins to glow
Even as a dying coal
revives with wind"?

(27) Shakespeare's secretary.

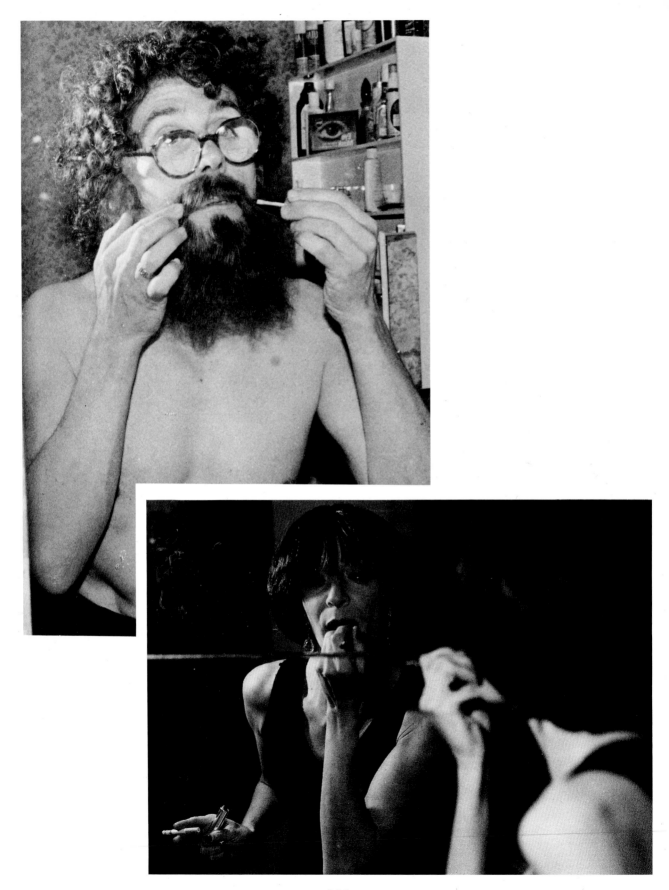

Christopher Lee as
CHARLEMAGNE

It turned out that Christopher Lee lives only two streets away from me so he phoned one day to say he was happy to come and do a picture, but who? He ran through a shortlist he'd written which included Imhotep and Genghis Khan among others. Eventually he decided upon Charlemagne, 'with whom,' he told me, 'I have a connection.'

I painted a background based on the interior of the church of St Mary at Aachen which the Holy Roman Emperor had had built, and in which he was buried in 814.

As Christopher was getting into his costume he told me about his connection with Charlemagne. 'I wear his arms on my great-grandfather's ring. We are from one of the six oldest families in Italy on my mother's side. My father's side is from this country – almost certainly gypsy with a name like Lee. I can only get back to 1400 with my father's side.

'When I was writing my book, the archivists found that Charlemagne had ennobled my family. Very probably there was a relationship, too. If you look at the face you see there is a strong similarity – even now, after a thousand or more years. It's the same with all my ancestors – long faces, long noses, dark eyes. Actually, Charlemagne was a Frank, he wasn't Italian. He was crowned Emperor of the Romans on Christmas Day AD 800 in St Peter's in Rome. He had a very high voice, for some reason. He was nearly as tall as I am, which was unusual in those days.

'His descendant, the Emperor Frederick Barbarossa, gave my family the right to wear his arms: the double-headed eagle.

'Actually,' confided Christopher, 'we go back a great deal earlier than that – long before him. We go back to the Romans.'

Sir Hugh Casson as
VOLTAIRE

'We have two choices here,' said Hugh, wondering aloud about his choice of character. 'I'm often mistaken for Michael Foot, but would you class him as being historical enough? It happens quite frequently, actually. Just the other day I was sitting in a taxi when someone came up, slapped the roof and said, "All right, Michael, mate?" – I've given up explaining that I am not Michael Foot and so I just said, "All right, mate," back and gave him a thumbs up.'

'No, we won't do Michael Foot. The other alternative is Voltaire – he's another person that I am supposed to resemble. I rather like the idea of wearing the long red dressing-gown.

'He probably wrote long into the night, straining to see the paper in the dim light from a candle – he would have been hunched over it, like this. Wasn't he particularly ugly? I can't remember any contemporary portraits, but I seem to think he had a very screwed-up old face and was probably fairly miserable most of the time.

'He was actually a man of great sensibility if I remember my history lessons correctly. He was logical too. And would not suffer fools. That's what made him unpopular with so many people (who were probably fools themselves, and resented being recognised as such).

'Wasn't it Voltaire who said, "There are no sects in geometry"? A good observation. He's saying that in such a pure science as geometry there can be no conflicting dogmas (unlike the confusion that abounds with ethics and morals). It's either right or it's bloody well wrong! I like that.'

118

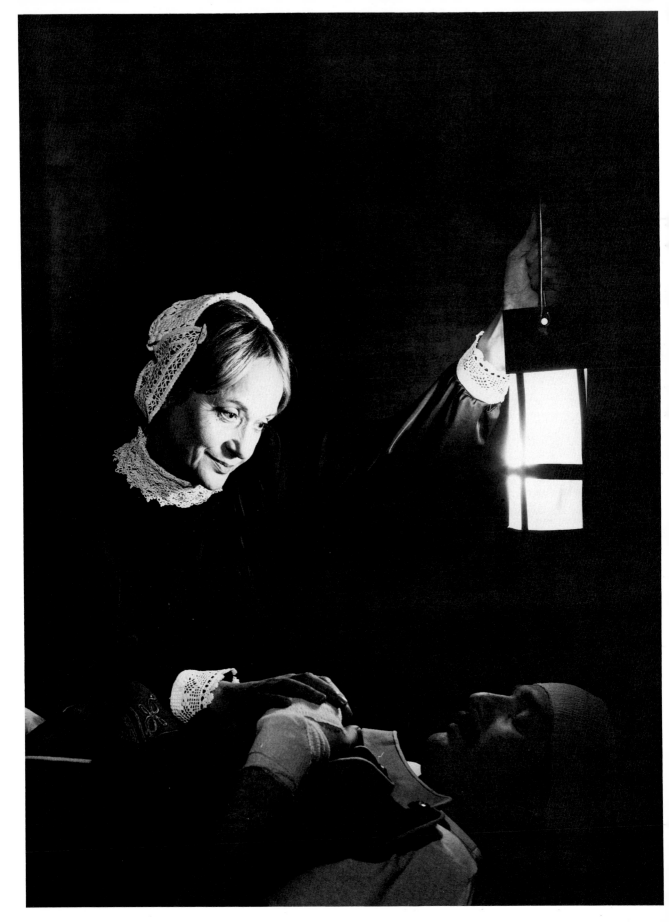

Sylvia Syms as
FLORENCE NIGHTINGALE

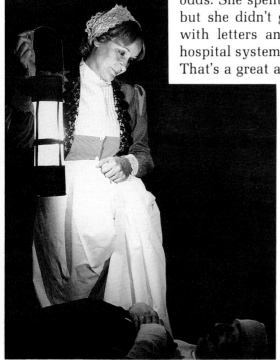

'I suppose we should go for the well-known image of her as angel of mercy in the Crimea,' said Sylvia on the phone to me. 'Do you know any wounded soldiers?'

'As a matter of fact, I do,' I answered and enlisted the help of a friend to lie dying on the bed.

'Actually, Crimea only took up a small part of her life but it's the part the history books find most romantic – though I'm sure it was a horrendous experience. She must have come across the most dreadful injuries of war. It was most unusual for any woman to be right there in the midst of battle at that time. I think she was a very practical woman, which I like to think I am as well. By all accounts she was also somewhat forbidding – which I hope I'm not.

'She did a lot of good work. The thing I admire most, I suppose, is her determination and perseverance against all odds. She spent the last years of her life confined to bed, but she didn't give up. She bombarded the government with letters and when she died she had reformed the hospital system into the beginnings of what we have now. That's a great achievement to be remembered for.'

Burt Kwouk as
SUN YAT SEN

'The bell rang and I answered the front door. There stood a dark figure in lumberjack coat and small peaked cap.

'Anthony? Burt,' said the figure, extending a friendly hand (the same hand that had threatened the neck and other parts of Inspector Clouseau whenever he had gone to the fridge or to run a bath).

'Are you hungry?' I asked, for it was early in the day.

'Actually, now you ask,' said Burt, 'I'd rather enjoy some toast and honey.'

One piece of toast and honey later I asked if he would like another and he said yes, he would.

This happened six times.

All this eating of toast and honey gave him ample time to fill me in on his choice of Sun Yat Sen.

'Well, when you asked me, I first thought of the obvious oriental ones like Genghis Khan, or the Dowager Empress but then I thought, "let's try someone a little more obscure and have a history lesson at the same time." Actually, there *is* a connection between us. Sun's ancestors came from a district called Chung San, which is a collection of villages and is part of the Guang Dong province.' He chewed his toast and swallowed. 'So did my ancestors, about five generations back on my father's side.

'Sun, as you know, was a revolutionary and there is something about him that appeals to me. He is one of the few figures from modern history whose reputation has survived pretty well unsullied. Others seem to yo-yo up and down in popular opinion depending on the mood of the day. There are few existing photos of him but I think his head was wider than mine. It doesn't matter.'

The sitting completed, the dark figure in lumberjack coat and peaked cap wandered off inscrutably in the direction of the Tube station.

Nick Owen and Anne Diamond as
ANTONY AND CLEOPATRA

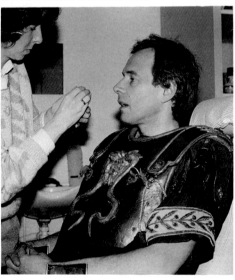

I trundled my way to Camden Town and parked in the TV-AM car park. Outside the building stood a small group of eager-looking people obviously awaiting the exit of 'someone famous'. This turned out to be the newest formation of the Osmond family (remember them?). Out came Mommy and Daddy followed by a clutch of lookalike children ranging from small to barely visible who followed behind them like ducklings on the Serpentine, all in matching satin bomber jackets.

I walked past this amusing sight into the main reception area where a girl at the desk gave me a piece of sticky paper with Mr Grant written on it and told me not to put it on anything leather so I didn't.

Another person came and took me up some spidery stairs, and back down the spidery stairs, along a dark corridor and into 'the place you'll be taking the photograph' which turned out to be the studio containing *that* settee upon which have sat a myriad famous bottoms.

I went along to the make-up department where I discovered Anne and Nick being groomed and powdered and laughing with glee at their costumes.

'Isn't this wonderful?' said Anne into her mirror.

'Yes,' said Nick, receiving an untimely mouthful of powder.

Then it was with the regal elegance due to the event that we passed along the corridor back to the studio.

I figured Anne should, as voluptuous queen, be seated upon her burnished throne while Nick, as horny Triumvir, should be appealing and panting all around. He seemed to have difficulty perching on the side of the chair – something about his helmet being in the way.

Try as I would, the scene soon deteriorated into

frolicsome mayhem with people coming in for a 'quick look' until soon a crowd of some proportion had formed behind me. And here's me trying to take a serious photograph!

It was certainly different from the usual sittings. Excitement and guffaws of laughter all around.

'Break open the TV-AM bottle of wine!' someone shouted.

'If only we knew where they kept it,' came the anguished reply.

A few weeks later I appeared on TV-AM's 'After Nine' with Jayne Irving, and showed the finished photograph.

'Why did you choose Cleopatra?' Anne was asked.

'So many reasons. I've always fancied trying that wonderful make-up and dressing in those blue and gold Egyptian clothes. Queen for a day! It gave us a chance to see Nick's knees as well. What a performance!'

And why did Nick choose Antony?

'Well, she told me to, didn't she?'

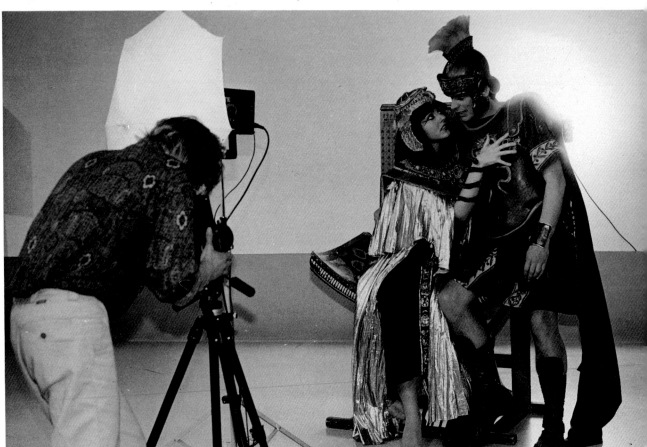

Spike Milligan as
RONALD REAGAN

Spike's face is enough for me. He doesn't have to say a word to send me into fits of helpless laughter.

He is the living paradox of the genuinely funny man with serious things to say. I don't think most people know how to accept him. Do you take his solemnity twice as seriously as that of the permanently serious man? Or do you reject his words as trite, coming as they do from someone who can find the ridiculous in anything?

'I hate photographers who ask me to pull silly faces,' he told me. 'Why should I if I don't feel like it? Do you know what I do when they ask? I just smile at them and think to myself "you ***! You ****** stupid ***". But I hope you don't think I'm being rude. I didn't mean you.'

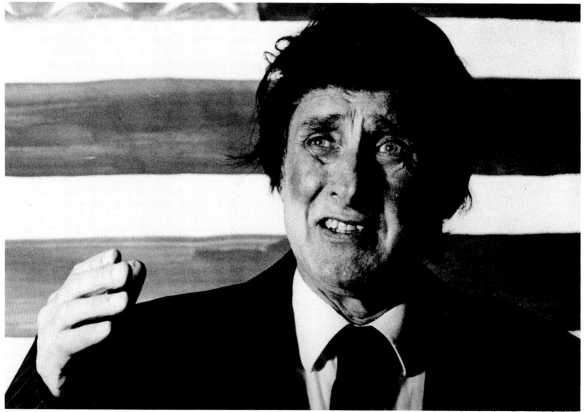

Minutes later, he was applying his wife's rouge to his cheeks in thick dabs and assuming the role (and the wig) of the United States' oldest living President.

'Here's the shaky wave he does when he can't think of anything to say.

'How about this? This is when someone asks him a difficult question and he doesn't know the answer so he just smiles.

'I'll do one now that I bet your publisher won't print. Reagan often shuts his eyes when he's thinking hard for a reply. They won't print it, because they'll think I blinked.'

I asked Spike what made him choose Ronald Reagan.

'I'm too tall for Toulouse-Lautrec.'

This was the first time I had ever met Milligan and he was all that I had expected. A man whose humour seems at times a translucent veil barely obscuring a melancholy view of the world.

As I put away my cameras he sat at the piano and played some jazz which echoed around his grand house. 'This is real music,' he said.

On the piano stood a frame. In the frame was a picture.

In the picture a small dog cocked its leg against a neatly-trimmed hedge.

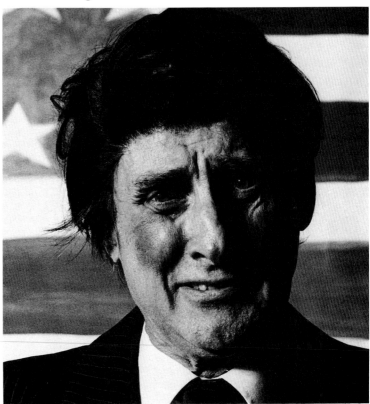

Ronald Ferguson as
MARCO POLO

The first time I met Ronald Ferguson he was sitting behind his desk at the Guards Polo Club in Windsor being bombarded with questions ('just for the record') concerning the background details to a certain forthcoming wedding. I was there to take pictures and, in my concentration, caught only snippets of the wonderfully tactful answers and vague deflections that he was giving to his inquisitors.

Around the office a smattering of pictures of various horses and Royals did little to break up the whiteness of the walls. It was not a plush office. It was a working office, where frames which hung askew were left like that until someone happened to notice, which didn't seem to be often. The desk was cluttered and the telephone was hot from ringing so much.

One question had the Major stumped. He thought and thought but the answer eluded him. I think it was the maiden name of a distant ancestor or something. He phoned his daughter Jane in Australia who told him the answer and the problem was solved.

Two days later I was on my hands and knees at the family house in Dummer, searching through the photograph albums for more 'background material'. I mentioned my book to Mrs Ferguson, and it turned out that she too had been doing a lot of charity work for hospitals. I hesitantly asked her the likelihood of the Major taking part in my project, and she immediately urged me to contact him about it – the idea of him in historical attire obviously a thing to be gleefully encouraged.

The result was Marco Polo.

'Print "POLO" in capital letters so everyone gets the connection,' said the tall figure struggling into what

appeared to be an ill-fitting dress which he wore under the fur cloak.

'You will never live this down,' I said, taking pictures as rapidly as I could.

'Nonsense,' he said, laughing. 'I've often had to wear a dress to a party – it's great fun. I like this wig, it's exactly the colour my hair used to be. What a hat! It's more like a frying pan or an omelette.'

In the studio he adopted some characteristic poses. 'I should be pointing to some new far-off land that I've just discovered. That's another connection I have with him; he was a traveller and explorer and my job has taken me all over the world to various exotic locations. Is that a good enough reason?

'Perhaps I should try and look more arrogant – my friends would tell me that's easy. He brought back lots of new spices – I should be looking quizically at them, perhaps inventing a name for them.'

I had previously photographed Major Ferguson on the morning of the wedding of the Duke and Duchess of York as he waited, cool as a cucumber, for the car to take him and his family to Clarence House for the start of the day's ceremony. As I looked at him now, sitting on an old trunk, dressed in a fur cloak and red wig, with pieces of his beard casually dropping off into his bowl of rice, it was difficult, but fun, to realise these two men were one and the same.

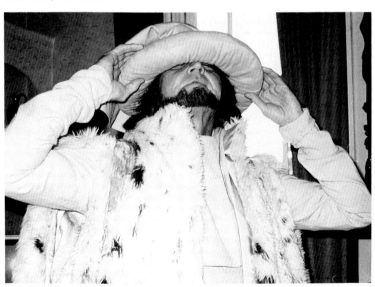

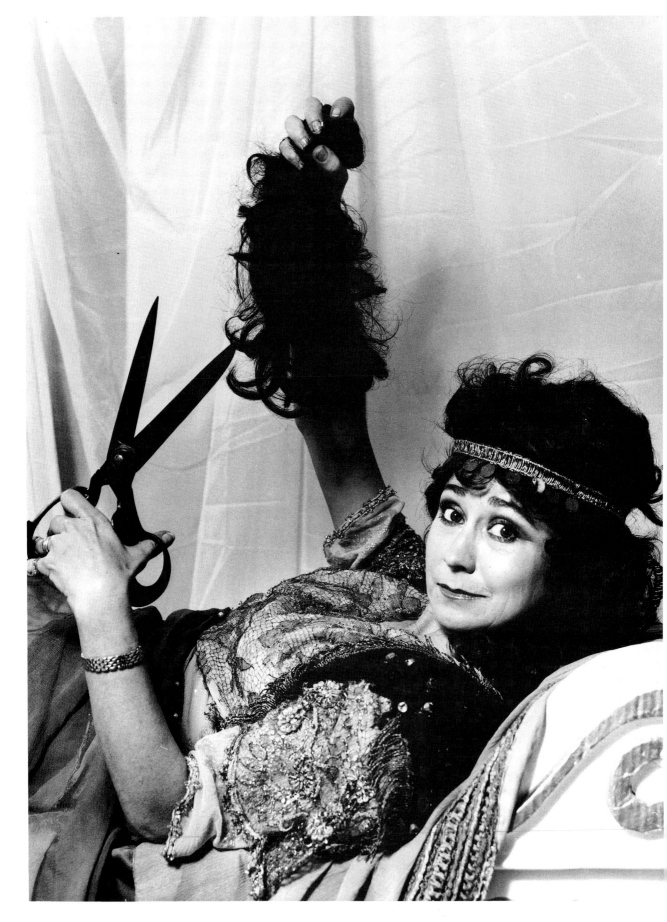

Felicity Kendal as
DELILAH

'She wanted to know exactly what made him tick, which is just like a woman. But she was rather extreme in her method of finding out! Poor devil. He was a member of that sect that aren't allowed to cut their hair, what are they called? It's on the tip of my tongue, come on, what is it? Don't you *ever* read your Bible?' she beseeched me.

'Of course, I'm just not very good with names.'

'Anyway, whatever they're called, he was one. And he believed that his strength was in his hair. Now, as I say, it's perfectly natural for a girl to want to know all about her boyfriend but honestly, there is a limit! I think she just became obsessed with the challenge of finding out where his immense strength lay. So she turned on the feminine charms. I think I should have my eyes made up as black as coal. What's this – wallpaper scissors! Oh well, I suppose it would take something like this to cut through Samson's hair. Is this a belly dancer's outfit – it's quite naughty. Probably just what Delilah would have worn. This is fun!'

I shrewdly observed that this could well be the end of her own wholesome image – did she mind?

'Not at all. It was fun while it lasted. Cheers!' she said, raising her glass of water and puffing on her cigarette. 'People will think I'm on the gin!'

Delilah

Marjorie Proops as
THE FIRST CREATURE ON EARTH

Proops in a swamp! Whatever next? I asked the woman to whom so many turn for advice whether she felt any sympathy for or connection with that first whatever-it-was that popped its head from the primordial soup all those long years ago – presuming of course that this is how it all started, rather than with Eve.

'Well, the thought of me being the mother of all we know is appealing – what a lovely idea. Mind you, I'm not sure everyone would agree with that!

'The first creature (which, I might add, probably didn't look like I do in your picture) would have been an innocent. Unspoilt by all these goings-on we've been up to ever since. That's quite a nice idea, isn't it? At that point, things could have gone in any direction and I'd like to think I would have been optimistic about it. Otherwise I'd have given up there and then and where would we be now? Nowhere. You wouldn't be doing your book and I wouldn't be sitting in your studio up to my neck in mud!'

At this point I'd like to award a suitable medal to Marjorie who struggled into her set without a murmur of complaint (it was the most awkward and unwieldy thing I made during this whole project) and sat for nearly an hour on what was a very hot summer's day laughing (hysterically?) at her unusual predicament.

'Anything for the Royal Marsden,' she said. 'I had a big argument with a politician last week who was going to close down the early diagnostic department until I had a good go at him for being so thoughtless.'

Needless to say the department stayed open.

Gordon Honeycombe as
KING ARTHUR

I languished in the back seat of the sleek black car that had come to take me and Gordon on an assignment to Hampshire. He was writing a royal wedding book and I had been asked to take pictures.

From my impressive position in the back I felt truly regal and once or twice had to stop myself waving at some passing commoner. In the front passenger seat sat our man Honeycombe. I asked him who he would like to portray in my book.

'It would be nice to be a legend beyond one's lunchtime – or breakfast time!' 9.30 a.m. seemed to me to be far too early for such jokes.

'I would choose to be King Arthur. He was the earliest of British heroes, an ideal chap, and very idealised. His legend has been going strong for nearly two thousand years.'

A month later, fresh from reading the breakfast news, Honeycombe continued his Arthurian monologue in my studio. With spirit gum gleaming on his chin he spoke to his reflection in the mirror.

'The fact that his father was probably Roman, that he was never a king as such, more likely a main-line mercenary beset with quarrelsome henchmen, a faithless friend, an adulterous wife, a murderous son, and an interfering old wizard, doesn't matter overmuch. He must have had an interesting time.'

Indeed, I struggled to capture the feel of this poor man whose heart must surely have weighed heavy under such momentous strain.

'This photograph is all wrong of course,' said Gordon,

'looking as it does like an over-emotional moment from *Camelot*. The *real* Arthur probably looked more like Fred Flintstone.

'However,' he conceded, 'it is the legend that counts.'

Georgina Hale as
LUCREZIA BORGIA

Georgina ('George' to her friends) has a truly hypnotic deep, dark voice and she will laugh when she knows I describe it as such. Very sexy. Just like Lucrezia.

'If I had to sum poor old Lucrezia up in one line, I suppose it would have to be "Out of sight, out of mind",' she said. The implication was lost on me for a moment, so she extended her one line to a second: 'If he gets in the way, try poison.'

'Of course, *now*, the theory is that it was all her brother Cesare's doing and Lucrezia remained an innocent to all the devilish goings-on which seemed to befall any man who so much as looked upon her. It saves on divorce bills, of course, but is that really any way to carry on and how could she have remained totally untarnished?

'It was a very different world then – long gloomy corridors and dark recesses – plenty of places for things to go on unnoticed. She may have been the world's most evil poisoner – she may have been an angel – who knows? After all, look at the stories of her father's and her brother's attitudes and relationship towards her, perhaps she did develop the same sort of character.

'I'm enjoying this. I feel quite wicked.'

Patrick Moore as
ARISTOTLE

Patrick Moore is as awe-inspiring a sight as any heavenly body.

My spirits sank when confronted by this towering figure who looked down upon me with monocled eye, for I had built a setting to house a far lesser-proportioned man.

'Oh dear, I should have told you that I injured myself playing cricket last June and I've subsequently put on rather a lot of weight – but don't worry, I'll squeeze in somehow.'

And squeeze in he did.

'Aristotle!' he said, removing his jacket to reveal a pair of thick white braces and blue tie across which streaked Halley's comet. 'Well – he was a great thinker who tackled a great many subjects from philosophy to astronomy, though his ideas were later controverted by Copernicus and Galileo...'

Manoeuvring into his tortuous confinement with not a little difficulty, he continued.

'...He made important scientific and philosophical advances and, above all others, his influence was paramount for many centuries after his death. His strong belief was that science and philosophy should follow fact – he placed great emphasis on the direct observation of nature. Do you think I could have a glass of water?'

Having cooled Patrick down (for it must be pointed out that all this took place on a hot day) I finally got him into the set and began taking pictures.

Patrick was one of the first 'famous faces' ever to reply to my pleas for a photograph. Back in 1980 he sent me a dog-eared postcard which appeared to be as old as the typewriter he had used to send the message:

Dear Anthony
I am no artist, but your project sounds most interesting.

Anneka Rice as
ROBIN HOOD

'I shall leave you my green tights,' scribbled Anneka Rice in my visitors' book. And sure enough, to this day, they sit in the boot of my car waiting to turn into an emergency fan belt.

'What a great tree,' she squealed, looking at my modest arboreal efforts.

'Is it really strong?' she said.

'Well, er, actually...' Too late! She jumped up on to one of the 'branches'.

I had terrible visions of the whole thing collapsing around my ears. Broken legs, broken cameras. '*TV star sues penniless photographer for ruined career – unable to pay, he is sent to fester in gaol for twenty years.*'

The structure creaked and groaned, but miraculously held together, though I was sure I sensed it swaying.

With a desperate sense of urgency I clicked away, determined to finish before what I felt sure must be impending disaster.

'I was always a tomboy when I was small...' said Anneka gazing skywards, blissfully unaware of her teetering position.

'...I spent all my time up trees. That's why I chose Robin Hood. It rather appealed – the idea of hopping through the forest, crawling along ditches, hiding in the bracken, spending nights outside in the open. Of course I was *always* the heroine, saving lives and defeating the enemy.'

(All that, just to come to a sticky end in a Chelsea bedroom, I thought.)

'However, I can't claim any far-reaching insight into the philosophy of stealing from the rich to give to the poor.'

Sir Michael Hordern as
IZAAK WALTON

A keen fisherman, Michael immediately suggested posing as Walton, seventeeth-century author of *The Compleat Angler*.

Michael has a theory about what to do when you are having your photograph taken.

'Talk, talk and keep talking.'

A photographer's nightmare, you may think (as I did when he first told me this) but with Hordern it seems to work.

'My face just falls dead if I'm not saying anything,' he said. And say things he did.

'There's a picture of Walton on a river bank, by Arthur Rackham I think.

'I have to go to Rome for one day next week. I'd rather be at home. Heathrow gets me down, oh, I hate it so.

'Walton is full of misinformation on fish and fishing – but it is a great classic, so what does it matter? Perhaps he used to draw – I'll draw. In pensive mood.

> *Then my heart with pleasure fills*
> *And dances with the daffodils.*

'I'm sorry for people who deal with cameras – a hell of a mess of equipment.

'Here I am writing.
'W-R-I-T-I-N-G, writing.
'I am writing,' (he sings to the tune of 'I Am Sailing').
'There's a poem I say at after-dinner speeches:

> Upon a river's bank serene
> A fisher sat where all was green
> And looked it.
> Anon, when light was growing dim
> He saw a fish (or else a fish saw him)
> And hooked it.
> He took with high-erected comb
> The fish (or else the story) home
> And cooked it.
> Recording angels by his bed
> Weighed all that he had done and said
> And booked it.

'Anon. Twentieth-century.' He laughed. 'It hides a germ of truth.'

Connie Booth as
LIZZIE BORDEN

Lizzie Borden took an axe
And gave her mother forty whacks;
When she saw what she had done,
She gave her father forty-one!

'I suppose I'm attracted by the paradox of the good little rich girl gone bad. I think the story would make a good opera. Lizzie was a well bred and dutiful daughter from an old Boston family. I think her father was an undertaker – anyway, he married beneath himself and was very mean to his daughter. Of course she killed them. But it's almost funny – she was totally respectable except for this one bizarre day – her defence was so strong that she got away with it and went on to live well afterwards – it's intriguing.'

Connie, being Connie, meant that Lizzie was soon reduced to a cross-eyed maniac, and once again I was laughing so much I found it difficult to take pictures.

'It's the transformation from sweet little girl to raving lunatic that I want to emphasise,' she said.

I had lunch with Connie some weeks later and showed her one of the more chilling photographs – a look of horror came over her face.

'I thought I was being funny – but look at this – it's so sinister.'

Lionel Jeffries as
ALBERT EINSTEIN

I don't know which of us was more amazed at the transformation when Lionel put on the spidery wig.

'My God,' he said, 'I'm his spitting image!'

A little burnt cork on the moustache, and the illusion was complete.

He sat at a desk littered with paper and started to scribble away in an Einsteinian frenzy. Pictures of atom bombs, baffling equations, a portrait of the man as mad professor.

'Einstein had this love/hate reaction to being a celebrity. He was irritated by all the attention from the newspapers and yet, at the same time, he would play-act for them. There's a great picture of him sticking his tongue out at a photographer who was obviously trying to get a crafty snap.

'He was probably a bit unhinged, don't you think? I'm sure all these geniuses have a screw or two loose. Too intelligent for their own good, so they go a little bit mad. Or even a lot mad. Can you imagine him writing out a shopping list for the wife?

'2 pints milk
½ pound potatoes
$E = MC^2$
and a packet of fags!'

Nigel Hawthorne as
THE LAST MAN IN
THE WORLD

I overheard my sister talking about me on the telephone to one of her friends.

'Anthony's got an atom-bomb in his room,' she said. 'Last week it was a mountain-top, and before that a swamp.'

I could imagine the look of puzzled disdain on the other end of the line.

I suppose the last man in the world need not necessarily be sitting under the bomb, but that was the way I'd visualised it when Nigel Hawthorne suggested the character.

He liked the set and the idea and cheerfully donned the torn suit, and blotted his face with burnt cork.

'What wonderfully ghastly wallpaper,' he said, examining the wall I'd constructed. 'It's like the stuff you find in a downtown Chinese restaurant.' I didn't tell him you could also find it all over the dining-room wall downstairs.

'Being the last man,' he said, 'would have its ups and downs, I suppose. At least you'd have time to read the paper in peace without being interrupted! Ah, tea. Does this look funny with me enjoying my cuppa under the shadow of the bomb? Oblivious to what's going on behind me...

'What was that?

'Did I hear something?

'I could be looking off into the distance as if I thought I just saw someone else... Hellooooo!

'Better still, I should look cross because there's a piece of plaster from the ceiling gone in my cup. Totally mad. I think you would have to be if you were the only person left. On second thoughts, I don't think I fancy this character much at all.'

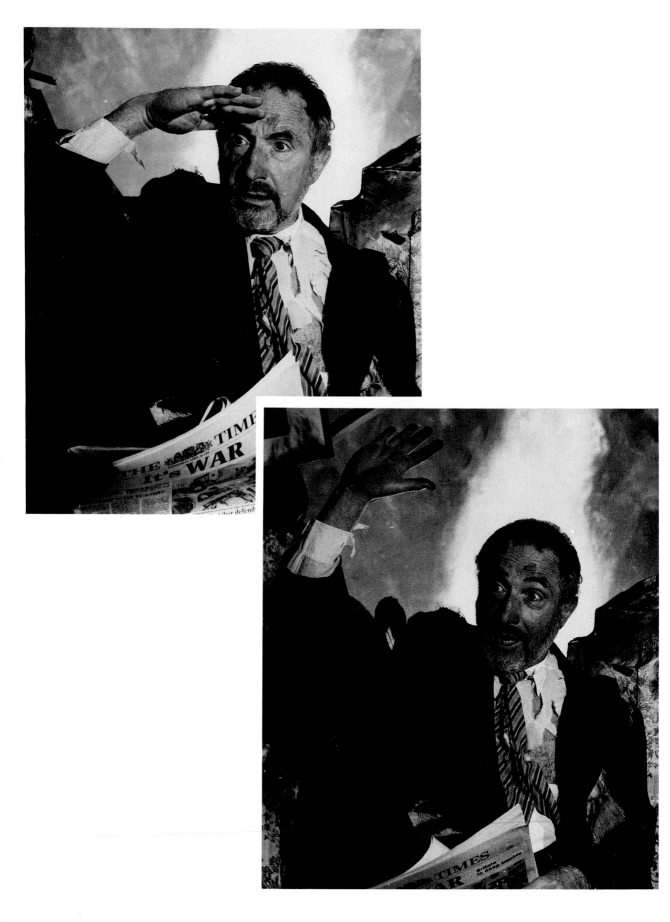